The Lost Keys of Freemasonry
Or
The Secret of Hiram Abiff

By Manly P. Hall

ISBN: 978-1-63118-427-7

Foundations of Freemasonry
Series

Other Books in this Series and Related Titles

Royal Arch, Capitular and Cryptic Masonry
by William F. Kuhn, William Potts George, High McCurdy and
Arthur Edward Waite (978-1-63118-425-3)

Ancient Mysteries and Secret Societies by Manly P. Hall
(978-1-63118-410-9)

Ancient Egyptian Mysteries and Hieroglyphics, Modern Freemasonry &
Initiation of the Pyramid by Henry Ridgely Evans, Manly P. Hall,
George Smith and Albert G. Mackey (978-1-63118-430-7)

Masonic Symbolism of the Apron & the Altar by Albert G. Mackey,
William Harvey, H. L. Haywood, Joseph Fort Newton
and H. A. Kingsbury (978-1-63118-428-4)

The Book of Parables by Enoch (978-1-63118-429-1)

Symbolism of the Corner Stone, the North East Corner and the Religious &
Masonic Symbolism of Stones by Albert G. Mackey, William Harvey
and William Wynn Westcott (978-1-63118-412-3)

Rosicrucian and Masonic Origins by Manly P. Hall (978-1-63118-000-2)

The Philosophy of Masonry in Five Parts by Roscoe Pound
(978-1-63118-004-0)

The Story and Legend of Hiram Abiff by William Harvey, Manly P.
Hall and Albert G. Mackey (978-1-63118-411-6)

Symbolism and Discourses on the Entered Apprentice, Fellowcraft and
Master Mason Blue Lodge Degrees
by H. L. Haywood, Asahel W. Gage, William Harvey, Albert G.
Mackey and Arthur Edward Waite (978-1-63118-413-0)

Audio Versions are also Available on Audible and iTunes

Table of Contents

Series Introduction...7

Introduction...9

Prologue: In the Fields of Chaos...17

Temple Builders...25

Chapter I: The Eternal Quest...27

Thoughtlessness...35

Chapter II: The Candidate...37

Chapter III: The Entered Apprentice...45

Chapter IV: The Fellow Craft...55

Chapter V: The Master Mason...61

Transmutation...67

The Presence of the Master...69

Chapter VI: The Qualifications of a True Mason...71

Masons, Awake!...79

Epilogue: Motive...81

Introduction

From the beginning of Modern Freemasonry's birthdate of 1717, the intelligentsia of humanity have found refuge for safe reflection within the walls of the fraternity. Masonic writers have produced a nearly incalculable amount of written musings on a multitude of esoteric and philosophical subjects, as they relate to the ancient mysteries that Freemasonry currently storehouses. Sadly, most of it appears to have sat largely unread, as American Freemasonry in particular, continues to transform itself into something that bears little resemblance to what it was originally designed to be. The true essence of Freemasonry is not that of blind patriotism or a single-minded national religion but one of Universal Brotherhood and altruism, designed for the betterment not just of its members but of society as a whole. In particular, for those who are not members of the fraternity, as Freemasonry has always acted as a beacon, to help guide humanity through darker times, with the hopes that one day we will collectively reach a truly enlightened age.

It's not uncommon for new members joining the fraternity to find little education within the walls of many modern lodges, in spite of so much written material available to the membership. Many older members are not simply uneducated with regards to real Masonic history and symbology, not to mention the vast arena of related subjects, but they are disinterested in all of it, as well.

Lamp of Trismegistus is doing its part to help preserve humanity's Masonic history by making some of these classics available to those students who are seeking to unearth the knowledge of these ancient colossi. As such, Lamp of Trismegistus offers its readers highlights of Masonic study, culled from a variety of authors and viewpoints, with the hope bringing education back into the fraternity. So, be sure to check out other titles in our *Foundations of Freemasonry Series* as well as our *Esoteric Classics*, *Theosophical Classics*, *Occult Fiction* and our *Christian Apocrypha Series*, and don't be afraid to let a little altruism into your own heart or even into your Lodge. You can also download the audio versions of most of these titles from iTunes or Audible.

The Lost Keys of Freemasonry

INTRODUCTION

Freemasonry, though not a religion, is essentially religious. Most of its legends and allegories are of a sacred nature; much of it is woven into the structure of Christianity. We have learned to consider our own religion as the only inspired one, and this probably accounts for much of the misunderstanding in the world today concerning the place occupied by Freemasonry in the spiritual ethics of our race. A religion is a divinely inspired code of morals. A religious person is one inspired to nobler living by this code. He is identified by the code which is his source of illumination. Thus we may say that a Christian is one who receives his spiritual ideals of right and wrong from the message of the Christ, while a Buddhist is one who molds his life into the archetype of morality given by the great Gautama, or one of the other Buddhas. All doctrines which seek to unfold and preserve that invisible spark in man named Spirit, are said to be spiritual. Those which ignore this invisible element and concentrate entirely upon the visible are said to be material. There is in religion a wonderful point of balance, where the materialist and spiritist meet on the plane of logic and reason. Science and theology are two ends of a single truth, but the world will never receive the full benefit of their investigations until they have made peace with each other, and labor hand in hand for the accomplishment of the great work - the liberation of spirit and intelligence from the three-dimensional prison-house of ignorance, superstition, and fear. That which gives man a knowledge of himself can be inspired only by the Self - and God is the Self in all things. In truth, He is the inspiration and the thing inspired. It has been stated in Scripture that God was the Word and that the Word was made flesh. Man's task now is to make flesh reflect the glory of that Word, which is within the soul of himself. It is this task which has created the need of religion - not one faith alone but many creeds, each searching in its own way, each meeting the needs of individual people, each emphasizing one point above all the others.

Twelve Fellow Craftsmen are exploring the four points of the compass. Are not these twelve the twelve great world religions, each seeking in its own way for that which was lost in the ages past, and the quest of which is the birthright of man? Is not the quest for Reality in a world of illusions the task for which each comes into the world? We are here to gain balance in a sphere of unbalance; to find rest in a restless thing; to unveil illusion; and to slay the dragon of our own animal natures. As David, King of Israel, gave to the hands of his son Solomon the task he could not accomplish, so each generation gives to the next the work of building the temple, or rather, rebuilding the dwelling of the Lord, which is on Mount Moriah.

Truth is not lost, yet it must be sought for and found. Reality is ever-present - dimensionless yet all-prevailing. Man - creature of attitudes and desires, and servant of impressions and opinions - cannot, with the wavering unbalance of an untutored mind, learn to know that which he himself does not possess. As man attains a quality, he discovers that quality, and recognizes about him the thing newborn within himself. Man is born with eyes, yet only after long years of sorrow does he learn to see clearly and in harmony with the Plan. He is born with senses, but only after long experience and fruitless strivings does he bring these senses to the temple and lays them as offerings upon the altar of the great Father, who alone does all things well and with understanding. Man is, in truth, born in the sin of ignorance, but with a capacity for understanding. He has a mind capable of wisdom, a heart capable of feeling, and a hand strong for the great work in life - truing the rough ashlar into the perfect stone.

What more can any creature ask than the opportunity to prove the thing he is, the dream that inspires him, the vision that leads him on? We have no right to ask for wisdom. In whose name do we beg for understanding? By what authority do we demand happiness? None of these things is the birthright of any creature; yet all may have them, if they will cultivate within themselves the thing that they desire. There is no need of asking, nor does any Deity bow down to give man these things that he desires. Man is given by Nature, a gift, and that gift is the privilege of labor. Through labor he learns all things.

Religions are groups of people, gathered together in the labor of learning. The world is a school. We are here to learn, and our presence here proves our need of instruction. Every living creature is struggling to break the strangling bonds of limitation - that pressing narrowness which inhabits vision and leaves the life without an ideal. Every soul is engaged in a great work - the labor of personal liberation from the state of ignorance. The world is a great prison; its bars are the Unknown. And each is a prisoner until, at last, he earns the right to tear these bars from their moldering sockets, and pass, illuminated and inspired, into the darkness, which becomes lighted by that presence. All peoples seek the temple where God dwells, where the spirit of the great Truth illuminates the shadows of human ignorance, but they know not which way to turn nor where this temple is. The mist of dogma surrounds them. Ages of thoughtlessness bind them in. Limitation weakens them and retards their footsteps. They wander in darkness seeking light, failing to realize that the Light is in the heart of the darkness.

To the few who have found Him, God is revealed. These, in turn, reveal Him to man, striving to tell ignorance the message of wisdom. But seldom does man understand the mystery that has been unveiled. He tries weakly to follow in the steps of those who have attained, but all too often finds the path more difficult than he even dreamed. So he kneels in prayer before the mountain he cannot climb, from whose top gleams the light which he is neither strong enough to reach nor wise enough to comprehend. He lives the law as he knows it, always fearing in his heart that he has not read aright the flaming letters in the sky, and that in living the letter of the Law he has murdered the spirit. Man bows humbly to the Unknown, peopling the shadows of his own ignorance with saints and saviors, ghosts and spectres, gods and demons. Ignorance fears all things, falling, terror-stricken before the passing wind. Superstition stands as the monument to ignorance, and before it kneel all who realize their own weakness; who see in all things the strength they do not possess; who give to sticks and stones the power to bruise them; who change the beauties of Nature into the dwelling place of ghouls and ogres. Wisdom fears no thing, but still bows humbly to its own Source. While superstition hates all things, wisdom, with its deeper understanding, loves all things; for it has seen the beauty, the tenderness, and the sweetness which underlie Life's mystery.

Life is the span of time appointed for accomplishment. Every fleeting moment is an opportunity, and those who are great are the ones who have recognized life as the opportunity for all things. Arts, sciences, and religions are monuments standing for what humanity has already accomplished. They stand as memorials to the unfolding mind of man, and through them man acquires more efficient and more intelligent methods of attaining prescribed results. Blessed are those who can profit by the experiences of others; who, adding to that which has already been built, can make their inspiration real, their dreams practical. Those who give man the things he needs, while seldom appreciated in their own age, are later recognized as the Saviors of the human race.

Masonry is a structure built upon experience. Each stone is a sequential step in the unfolding of intelligence. The shrines of Masonry are ornamented by the jewels of a thousand ages; its rituals ring with the words of enlightened seers and illuminated sages. A hundred religions have brought their gifts of wisdom to its altar. Arts and sciences unnumbered have contributed to its symbolism. It is more than a faith; it is a path of certainty. It is more than a belief; it is a fact. Masonry is a university, teaching the liberal arts and sciences of the soul to all who will attend to its words. It is a shadow of the great Atlantean Mystery School, which stood with all its splendor in the ancient City of the Golden Gates, where now the turbulent Atlantic rolls in unbroken sweep. Its chairs are seats of learning; its pillars uphold the arch of universal education, not only in material things, but also in those qualities which are of the spirit. Upon its trestleboards are inscribed the sacred truths of all nations and of all peoples, and upon those who understand its sacred depths has dawned the great Reality. Masonry is, in truth, that long-lost thing which all peoples have sought in all ages. Masonry is the common denominator as well as the common devisor of human aspiration.

Most of the religions of the world are like processions: one leads, and the many follow. In the footsteps of the demigods, man follows in his search for truth and illumination. The Christian follows the gentle Nazarene up the winding slopes of Calvary. The Buddhist follows his great emancipator through his wanderings in the wilderness. The Mohammedan makes his pilgrimage across the desert sands to the black tent at Mecca. Truth leads, and ignorance follows in his train. Spirit blazes the trail, and matter follows behind. In the world today ideals live but a moment in their purity, before the gathering hosts of darkness snuff out the gleaming spark. The Mystery School, however, remains unmoved. It does not bring its light to man; man must bring his light to it. Ideals, coming into the world, become idols within a few short hours, but man, entering the gates of the sanctuary, changes the idol back to an ideal.

Man is climbing an endless flight of steps, with his eyes fixed upon the goal at the top. Many cannot see the goal, and only one or two steps are visible before them. He has learned, however, one great lesson - namely, that as he builds his own character he is given strength to climb the steps. Hence a

Mason is a builder of the temple of character. He is the architect of a sublime mystery - the gleaming, glowing temple of his own soul. He realizes that he best serves God when he joins with the Great Architect in building more noble structures in the universe below. All who are attempting to attain mastery through constructive efforts are Masons at heart, regardless of religious sect or belief. A Mason is not necessarily a member of a lodge. In a broad sense, he is any person who daily tries to live the Masonic life, and to serve intelligently the needs of the Great Architect. The Masonic brother pledges himself to assist all other temple-builders in whatever extremity of life; and in so doing he pledges himself to every living thing, for they are all temple- builders, building more noble structures to the glory of the universal God.

The true Masonic Lodge is a Mystery School, a place where candidates are taken out of the follies and foibles of the world and instructed in the mysteries of life, relationships, and the identity of that germ of spiritual essence within, which is, in truth, the Son of God, beloved of His Father. The Mason views life seriously, realizing that every wasted moment is a lost opportunity, and that Omnipotence is gained only through earnestness and endeavor. Above all other relationships he recognizes the universal brotherhood of every living thing. The symbol of the clasped hands, explained in the Lodge, reflects his attitude towards all the world, for he is the comrade of all created things. He realizes also that his spirit is a glowing, gleaming jewel which he must enshrine within a holy temple built by the labor of his hands, the meditation of his heart, and the aspiration of his soul.

Freemasonry is a philosophy which is essentially creedless. It is the truer for it. Its brothers bow to truth regardless of the bearer; they serve light, instead of wrangling over the one who brings it. In this way they prove that they are seeking to know better the will and the dictates of the Invincible One. No truer religion exists than that of world comradeship and brotherhood, for the purpose of glorifying one God and building for Him a temple of constructive attitude and noble character.

PROLOGUE

IN THE FIELDS OF CHAOS

The first flush of awakening Life pierced the impenetrable expanse of Cosmic Night, turning the darkness of negation into the dim twilight of unfolding being. Silhouetted against the shadowy gateways of Eternity, the lonely figure of a mystic stranger stood upon the nebulous banks of swirling substance. Robed in a shimmery blue mantle of mystery and his head encircled by a golden crown of dazzling light, the darkness of Chaos fled before the rays that poured like streams of living fire from his form divine.

From some Cosmos greater far than ours this mystic visitor came, answering the call of Divinity. From star to star he strode and from world to universe he was known, yet forever concealed by the filmy garments of chaotic night. Suddenly the clouds broke and a wondrous light descended from somewhere among the seething waves of force; it bathed this lonely form in a radiance celestial, each sparkling crystal of mist gleaming like a diamond bathed in the living fire of the Divine.

In the gleaming flame of cosmic light bordered by the dark clouds of not-being two great forms appeared and a mighty Voice thrilled eternity, each sparkling atom pulsating with the power of the Creator's Word while the great blue-robed figure bowed in awe before the foot-stool of His Maker as a hand reached down from heaven, its fingers extended the benediction.

"Of all creation I have chosen you and upon you my seal is placed. You are the chosen instrument of my hand and I appoint you to be the Builder of my Temple. You shall raise its pillars and tile its floor; you shall ornament it with metals and with jewels and you shall be the master of my workmen. In your hands I place the plans and here on the tracing board of living substance I have impressed the plan you are to follow, tracing its every letter and angle in the fiery lines of my moving finger. Hiram Abiff, chosen builder of your Father's house, up and to your work. Yonder are the fleecy clouds, the gray mists of dawn, the gleams of heavenly light, and the darkness of the sleep of creation. From these shall you build, without the sound of hammer or the voice of workmen, the temple of your God, eternal in the heavens. The swirling, ceaseless motion of negation you shall chain to grind your stones. Among these spirits of not-being shall you slack your lime and lay your footings; for I have watched you through the years of your youth; I have guided you through the days of your manhood. I have weighed you in the balance and you have not been found wanting. Therefore, to you give I the glory of work, and here ordain you as the Builder of my House. Unto you I give the word of the Master Builder; unto you I give the tools of the craft; unto you I give the power that has been vested in me. Be faithful unto these things. Bring them back when you have finished, and I will give you the name known to God alone. So mote it be."

The great light died out of the heavens, the streaming fingers of living light vanished in the misty, lonely twilight, and again covered not-being with its sable mantle. Hiram Abiff again stood alone, gazing out into the endless ocean of oblivion - nothing but swirling, seething matter as far as eye could see. Then he straightened his shoulders and, taking the trestleboard in his hands and clasping to his heart the glowing Word of the Master, walked slowly away and was swallowed up in the mists of primordial dawn.

How may man measure timeless eternity? Ages passed, and the lonely Builder labored with his plan with only love and humility in his heart, his hand molding the darkness which he blessed while his eyes were raised above where the Great Light had shone down from heaven. In the divine solitude he labored, with no voice to cheer, no spirit to condemn - alone in the boundless all with the great chill of the morning mist upon his brow, but his heart still warm with the light of the Master's Word. It seemed a hopeless task. No single pair of hands could mold that darkness; no single heart, no matter how true, could be great enough to project pulsing cosmic love into the cold mist of oblivion. Though the darkness settled ever closer about him and the misty fingers of negation twined round his being, still with divine trust the Builder labored; with divine hope he laid his footings, and from the boundless clay he made the molds to cast his sacred ornaments. Slowly the building grew and dim forms molded by the Master's hand took shape about him. Three huge, soulless creatures had the Master fashioned, great beings which loomed like grim spectres in the semi-darkness. They were three builders he had blessed and now in stately file they passed before him, and Hiram held out his arms to his creation, saying, "Brothers, I have built you for your works. I have formed you to labor with me in the building of the Master's house. You are the children of my being; I have labored with you, now labor with me for the glory of our God."

But the spectres laughed. Turning upon their maker and striking him with his own tools given him by God out of heaven, they left their Grand Master dying in the midst of his labors, broken and crushed by the threefold powers of cosmic night. As he lay bleeding at the feet of his handiwork the martyred Builder raised his eyes to the seething clouds, and his face was sweet with divine love and cosmic understanding as he prayed unto the Master who had sent him forth:

"O Master of Workmen, Great Architect of the universe, my labors are not finished. Why must they always remain undone? I have not completed the thing for which Thou hast sent me unto being, for my very creations have turned against me and the tools Thou gavest me have destroyed me. The children that I formed in love, in their ignorance have murdered me. Here, Father, is the Word Thou gavest me now red with my own blood. O Master, I return it to Thee for I have kept it sacred in my heart. Here are the tools, the tracing board, and the vessels I have wrought. Around me stand the ruins of my temple which I must leave. Unto Thee, O God, the divine Knower of all things, I return them all, realizing that in Thy good time lies the fulfillment of all things. Thou, O God, knowest our down-sitting and our uprising and Thou understandest our thoughts afar off. In Thy name, Father, I have labored and in Thy cause I die, a faithful builder."

The Master fell back, his upturned face sweet in the last repose of death, and the light rays no longer pouring from him.

The gray clouds gathered closer as though to form a winding sheet around the body of their murdered Master.

Suddenly the heavens opened again and a shaft of light bathed the form of Hiram in a glory celestial. Again the Voice spoke from the heavens where the Great King sat upon the clouds of creation: "He is not dead; he is asleep. Who will awaken him? His labors are not done, and in death he guards the sacred relics more closely than ever, for the Word and the tracing board are his - I have given them to him. But he must remain asleep until these three who have slain him shall bring him back to life, forever a wrong must be righted, and the slayers of my house, the destroyers of my temple, must labor in the place of their Builder until they raise their Master from the dead."

The three murderers fell on their knees and raised their hands to heaven as though to ward off the light which had disclosed their crime: "O God, great is our sin, for we have slain our Grand Master, Hiram Abiff! Just is Thy punishment and as we have slain him we now dedicate our lives to his resurrection. The first was our human weakness, the second our sacred duty."

"Be it so," answered the Voice from Heaven. The great Light vanished and the clouds of darkness and mist concealed the body of the murdered Master. It was swallowed up in the swirling darkness which left no mark, no gravestone to mark the place where the Builder had lain.

"O God!" cried the three murderers, "where shall we find our Master now?"

A hand reached down again from the Great Unseen and a tiny lamp was handed them, whose oil flame burned silently and clearly in the darkness. "By this light shall ye seek him whom ye have slain."

The three forms surrounded the light and bowed in prayer and thanksgiving for this solitary gleam which was to light the darkness of their way. From somewhere above in the regions of not-being the great Voice spoke, a thundering Voice that filled Chaos with its sound: "He cometh forth as a flower and is cut down; he teeth also as a shadow and continueth not; as the waters fail from the sea and the flood decayeth and drieth up, so man lieth down and riseth not again. Yet have I compassion upon the children of my creation; I administer unto them in time of trouble and save them with an everlasting salvation. Seek ye where the broken twig lies and the dead stick molds away, where the clouds float together and the stones rest by the hillside, for all these mark the grave of Hiram who has carried my Will with him to the tomb. This eternal quest is yours until ye have found your Builder, until the cup giveth up its secret, until the grave giveth up its ghosts. No more shall I speak until ye have found and raised my beloved Son, and have listened to the words of my Messenger and with Him as your guide have finished the temple which I shall then inhabit. Amen."

The gray dawn still lay asleep in the arms of darkness. Out through the great mystery of not-being all was silence, unknowable. Through the misty dawn, like strange phantoms of a dream, three figures wandered over the great Unknown carrying in their hands a tiny light, the lamp given to them by their Builder's Father. Over stick and stone and cloud and star they wandered, eternally in search of a silent grave, stopping again and again to explore the depths of some mystic recess, praying for liberation from their endless search; yet bound by their vows to raise the Builder they had slain, whose grave was marked by the broken twig, and whose body was laid away in the white winding sheet of death somewhere over the brow of the eternal hill.

TEMPLE BUILDERS

You are the temple builders of the future. With your hands must be raised the domes and spires of a coming civilization. Upon the foundation you have laid, tomorrow shall build a far more noble edifice. Builders of the temple of character wherein should dwell an enlightened spirit; truers of the rock of relationship; molders of those vessels created to contain the oil of life: up, and to the task appointed! Never before in the history of men have you had the opportunity that now confronts you. The world waits - waits for the illuminated one who shall come from between the pillars of the portico. Humility, hoodwinked and bound, seeks entrance to the temple of wisdom. Fling wide the gate, and let the worthy enter. Fling wide the gate, and let the light that is the life of men shine forth. Hasten to complete the dwelling of the Lord, that the Spirit of God may come and dwell among His people, sanctified and ordained according to His law.

CHAPTER I

THE ETERNAL QUEST

The average Mason, as well as the modern student of Masonic ideals, little realizes the cosmic obligation he takes upon himself when he begins his search for the sacred truths of Nature as they are concealed in the ancient and modern rituals. He must not lightly regard his vows, and if he would not bring upon himself years and ages of suffering he must cease to consider Freemasonry solely as a social order only a few centuries old. He must realize that the ancient mystic teachings as perpetuated in the modern rites are sacred, and that powers unseen and unrecognized mold the destiny of those who consciously and of their own free will take upon themselves the obligations of the Fraternity.

Freemasonry is not a material thing: it is a science of the soul; it is not a creed or doctrine but a universal expression of the Divine Wisdom. The coming together of medieval guilds or even the building of Solomon's temple as it is understood today has little, if anything, to do with the true origin of Freemasonry, for Masonry does not deal with personalities. In its highest sense, it is neither historical nor archaeological, but is a divine symbolic language perpetuating under certain concrete symbols the sacred mysteries of the ancients. Only those who see in it a cosmic study, a life work, a divine inspiration to better thinking, better feeling, and better living, with the spiritual attainment of enlightenment as the end, and with the daily life of the true Mason as the means, have gained even the slightest insight into the true mysteries of the ancient rites.

The age of the Masonic school is not to be calculated by hundreds or even thousands of years, for it never had any origin in the worlds of form. The world as we see it is merely an experimental laboratory in which man is laboring to build and express greater and more perfect vehicles. Into this laboratory pour myriads of rays descending from the cosmic hierarchies. These mighty globes and orbs which focus their energies upon mankind and mold its destiny do so in an orderly manner, each in its own way and place, and it is the working of these mystic hierarchies in the universe which forms the pattern around which the Masonic school has been built, for the true lodge of the Mason is the universe. Freed of limitations of creed and sect, he stands a master of all faiths, and those who take up the study of Freemasonry without realizing the depth, the beauty, and the spiritual power of its philosophy can never gain anything of permanence from their studies. The age of the Mystery Schools can be traced by the student back to the dawn of time, ages and aeons ago, when the temple of the Solar Man was in the making. That was the first Temple of the King, and therein were given and laid down the true mysteries of the ancient lodge, and it was the gods of creation and the spirits of the dawn who first tiled the Master's lodge.

The initiated brother realizes that his so called symbols and rituals are merely blinds fabricated by the wise to perpetuate ideas incomprehensible to the average individual. He also realizes that few Masons of today know or appreciate the mystic meaning concealed within these rituals. With religious faith we perpetuate the form, worshiping it instead of the life, but those who have not recognized the truth in the crystallized ritual, those who have not liberated the spiritual germ from the shell of empty words, are not Masons, regardless of their physical degrees and outward honors.

In the work we are taking up it is not the intention to dwell upon the modern concepts of the Craft but to consider Freemasonry as it really is to those who know, a great cosmic organism whose true brothers and children are tied together not by spoken oaths but by lives so lived that they are capable of seeing through the blank wall and opening the window which is now concealed by the rubbish of materiality. When this is done and the mysteries of the universe unfold before the aspiring candidate, then in truth he discovers what Freemasonry really is. Its material aspects interest him no longer for he has unmasked the Mystery School which he is capable of recognizing only when he himself has spiritually become a member of it.

Those who have examined and studied its ancient lore have no doubt that Freemasonry, like the universe itself, which is the greatest of all schools, deals with the unfolding of a three-fold principle; for all the universe is governed by the same three kings who are called the builders of the Masonic temple. They are not personalities but principles, great intelligent energies and powers which in God, man, and the universe have charge of the molding of cosmic substance into the habitation of the living king , the temple built through the ages first of unconscious and then conscious effort on the part of every individual who is expressing in his daily life the creative principles of these three kings.

The true brother of the ancient Craft realized that the completion of the temple he was building to the King of the Universe was a duty or rather a privilege which he owed to his God, to his brother, and to himself. He knew that certain steps must be taken and that his temple must be built according to the plan. Today it seems that the plan is lost, however, for in the majority of cases Freemasonry is no longer an operative art but is merely a speculative idea until each brother, reading the mystery of his symbols and pondering over the beautiful allegories unfolded in his ritual, realizes that he himself contains the keys and the plans so long lost to his Craft and that if he would ever learn Freemasonry he must unlock its doors with the key wrought from the base metals of his own being.

True Freemasonry is esoteric; it is not a thing of this world. All that we have here is a link, a doorway, through which the student may pass into the unknown. Freemasonry has nothing to do with things of form save that it realizes form is molded by and manifests the life it contains. Consequently the student is seeking so to mold his life that the form will glorify the God whose temple he is slowly building as he awakens one by one the workmen within himself and directs them to carry out the plan that has been given him out of heaven.

So far as it is possible to discover, ancient Freemasonry and the beautiful cosmic allegories that it teaches, perpetuated through hundreds of lodges and ancient mysteries, forms the oldest of the Mystery Schools; and its preservation through the ages has not depended upon itself as an exoteric body of partly evolved individuals but upon a concealed brotherhood, the exoteric side of Freemasonry. All the great mystery, Schools have hierarchies upon the spiritual planes of Nature which are expressing themselves in this world through creeds and organizations. The true student seeks to lift himself from the exoteric body upward spiritually until he joins the esoteric group which, without a lodge on the physical plane of Nature, is far greater than all the lodges of which it is the central fire. The spiritual instructors of humanity are forced to labor in the concrete world with things comprehensible to the concrete mind, and there man begins to comprehend the meaning of the allegories and symbols which surround his exoteric work as soon as he prepares himself to receive them. The true Mason realizes that the work of the Mystery Schools in the world is of an inclusive rather than an exclusive nature, and that the only lodge which is broad enough to express his ideals is one whose dome is the heavens, whose pillars are the corners of creation, whose checker-board floor is composed of the crossing currents of human emotion and whose altar is the human heart. Creeds cannot bind the true seeker for truth. Realizing the unity of all truth, the Mason also realizes that the hierarchies laboring with him have given him in his varying degrees the mystic spiritual rituals of all the Mystery Schools in the world, and if he would fill his place in the plan he must not enter this sacred study for what he can get out of it but that he may learn how to serve.

In Freemasonry is concealed the mystery of creation, the answer to the problem of existence, and the path the student must tread in order to join those who are really the living powers behind the thrones of modern national and international affairs. The true student realizes most of all that the taking of degrees does not make a man a Mason. A Mason is not appointed; he is evolved and he must realize that the position he holds in the exoteric lodge means nothing compared to his position in the spiritual lodge of life. He must forever discard the idea that he can be told or instructed in the sacred Mysteries or that his being a member of an organization improves him in any way. He must realize that his duty is to build and evolve the sacred teachings in his own being: that nothing but his own purified being can unlock the door to the sealed libraries of human consciousness, and that his Masonic rites must eternally be speculative until he makes them operative by living the life of the mystic Mason. His karmic responsibilities increase with his opportunities. Those who are surrounded with knowledge and opportunity for self-improvement and make nothing of these opportunities are the lazy workmen who will be spiritually, if not physically, cast out of the temple of the king.

The Masonic order is not a mere social organization, but is composed of all those who have banded themselves together to learn and apply the principles of mysticism and the occult rites. They are (or should be) philosophers, sages and sober-minded individuals who have dedicated themselves upon the Masonic altar and vowed by all they hold dear that the world shall be better, wiser, and happier because they have lived. Those who enter these mystic rites and pass between the pillars seeking either prestige or commercial advantage are blasphemers, and while in this world we may count them as successful, they are the cosmic failures who have barred themselves out from the true rite whose keynote is unselfishness and whose workers have renounced the things of earth.

In ancient times many years of preparation were required before the neophyte was permitted to enter the temple of the Mysteries. In this way the shallow, the curious, the faint of heart, and those unable to withstand the temptations of life were automatically eliminated by their inability to meet the requirements for admission. The successful candidate who did pass between the pillars entered the temple, keenly realizing his sublime opportunity, his divine obligation, and the mystic privilege which he had earned for himself through years of special preparation. Only those are truly Masons who enter their temple in reverence, who seek not the ephemeral things of life but the treasures which are eternal, whose sole desire is to know the true mystery of the Craft that they may join as honest workmen those who have gone before as builders of the Universal Temple. The Masonic ritual is not a ceremony, but a life to be lived. Those alone are truly Masons who, dedicating their lives and their fortunes upon the altar of the living flame, undertake the construction of the one universal building of which they are the workmen and their God the living Architect. When we have Masons like this the Craft will again be operative, the flaming triangle will shine forth with greater lustre, the dead builder will rise from his tomb, and the Lost Word so long concealed from the profane will blaze forth again with the power that makes all things new.

In the pages that follow have been set down a number of thoughts for the study and consideration of temple builders, craftsmen and artisans alike. They are the keys which, if only read, will leave the student still in ignorance but, if lived, will change the speculative Masonry of today into the operative Masonry of tomorrow, when each builder, realizing his own place, will see things which he never saw before, not because they were not there but because he was blind. And there are none so blind as those who will not see.

THOUGHTLESSNESS

The noblest tool of the Mason is his mind, but its value is measured by the use made of it. Thoughtful in all things, the aspiring candidate to divine wisdom attains reality in sincere desire, in meditation, and in silence. Let the keynote of the Craft, and of the Ritual, be written in blazing letters:

THINK OF ME.

What is the meaning of this mystic maze of symbols, rites and rituals?

THINK!

What does life mean, with the criss-crossings of human relationship, the endless pageantry of qualities masquerading in a carnival of fools?

THINK!

What is the plan behind it all, and who the planner? Where dwells the Great Architect, and what is the tracing board upon which he designs?

THINK!

What is the human soul, and why the endless yearning to ends unknown, along pathways where each must wander unaccompanied? Why mind, why soul, why spirit, and in truth, why anything?

THINK!

Is there an answer? If so, where will the truth be found? Think, Brothers of the Craft, think deeply; for if truth exists, you have it, and if truth be within the reach of living creature, what other goal is worth the struggle?

CHAPTER II

THE CANDIDATE

There comes a time in the growth of every living individual thing when it realizes with dawning consciousness that it is a prisoner. While apparently free to move and have its being, the struggling life cognizes through ever greater vehicles its own limitations. It is at this point that man cries out with greater insistence to be liberated from the binding ties which, though invisible to mortal eyes, still chain him with bonds far more terrible than those of any physical prison.

Many have read the story of the prisoner of Chillon who paced back and forth in the narrow confines of his prison cell, while the blue waters rolled ceaselessly above his head and the only sound that broke the stillness of his eternal night was the constant swishing and lapping of the waves. We pity the prisoner in his physical tomb and we are sad at heart, for we know how life loves liberty. But there is one prisoner whose plight is far worse than those of earth. He has not even the narrow confines of a prison cell around Him; He cannot pace ceaselessly to and fro and wear ruts in the cobblestones of His dungeon floor. That eternal Prisoner is Life incarnate within the dark stone walls of matter, with not a single ray to brighten the blackness of His fate. He fights eternally, praying in the dark confines of gloomy walls for light and opportunity. This is the eternal Prisoner who, through the ceaseless ages of cosmic unfoldment, through forms unnumbered and species now unknown, strives eternally to liberate Himself and gain self conscious expression, the birthright of every created thing. He awaits the day when, standing upon the rocks that now form His shapeless tomb, He may raise His arms to heaven, bathed in the sunlight of spiritual freedom, free to join the sparkling atoms and dancing light-beings released from the bonds of prison wall and tomb.

Around Life - that wondrous germ in the heart of every living thing, that sacred Prisoner in His gloomy cell, that Master Builder laid away in the grave of matter - has been built the wondrous legend of the Holy Sepulchre. Under allegories unnumbered, the mystic philosophers of the ages, have perpetuated this wonderful story, and among the Craft Masons it forms the mystic ritual of Hiram, the Master Builder, murdered in his temple by the very builders who should have served him as he labored to perfect the dwelling place of his God.

Matter is the tomb. It is the dead wall of substance not yet awakened into the pulsating energies of Spirit. It exists in many degrees and forms, not only in the chemical elements which form the solids of our universe but in finer and more subtle substances. These, though expressing through emotion and thought, are still beings of the world of form. These substances form the great cross of matter which opposes the growth of all things and by opposition makes all growth possible. It is the great cross of hydrogen, nitrogen, oxygen, and carbon upon which even the life germ in protoplasm is crucified and suspended in agony. These substances are incapable of giving it adequate expression. The Spirit within cries out for freedom: freedom to be, to express, to manifest its true place in the Great Plan of cosmic unfoldment.

It is this great yearning within the heart of man which sends him slowly onward toward the gate of the Temple; it is this inner urge for greater understanding and greater light which brought into being through the law of necessity the great cosmic Masonic Lodge dedicated to those seeking union with the Powers of Light that their prison walls might be removed. This shell cannot be discarded: it must be raised into union with the Life; each dead, crystallized atom in the human body must be set vibrating and spinning to a higher rate of consciousness. Through purification, through knowledge, and through service to his fellow man the candidate sequentially unfolds these mystic properties, building better and more perfect bodies through which his higher life secures even greater manifestation. The expression of man through constructive thought, emotion, and action liberates the higher nature from bodies which in their crystallized states are incapable of giving him his natural opportunities.

In Freemasonry this crystallized substance of matter is called the grave and represents the Holy Sepulchre. This is the grave within which the lost Builder lies and with Him are the plans of the Temple and the Master's Word, and it is this builder, our Grand Master, whom we must seek and raise from the dead. This noble Son of Light cries out to us in every expression of matter. Every stick and stone marks His resting place, and the sprig of acacia promises that through the long winter of spiritual darkness when the sun does not shine for man, this Light still awaits the day of liberation when each one of us shall raise Him by the grip of the Grand Master, the true grip of a Master Mason. We cannot hear this Voice that calls eternally, but we feel its inner urge. A great unknown something pulls at our heartstrings. As the ages roll by, the deep desire to be greater, to live better, and to think God's thoughts, builds within ourselves the qualifications of a candidate who, when asked why he takes the path , would truly answer if he knew mentally the things he feels: "I hear a voice that cries out to me from flora and fauna, from the stones, from the clouds, from the very heaven itself. Each fiery atom spinning and twisting in Cosmos cries out to me with the voice of my Master. I can hear Hiram Abiff, my Grand Master, crying out in his agony, the agony of life hidden within the darkness of its prison walls, seeking for the expression which I have denied it, laboring, to bring closer the day of its liberation , and I have learned to know that I am responsible for those walls. My daily actions are the things which as ruffians and traitors are murdering my God."

There are many legends of the Holy Sepulchre which for so many centuries had been in the hands of the infidel and which the Christian worlds sought to retake in the days of the Crusades. Few Masons realize that this Holy Sepulchre, or tomb, is in reality negation and crystallization - matter that has sealed within itself the Spirit of Life which must remain in darkness until the growth of each individual being gives it walls of glowing gold and changes its stones into windows. As we develop better and better vehicles of expression, these walls slowly expand until at last Spirit rises triumphant from its tomb and, blessing the very walls that confined it, raises them to union with itself.

We may first consider the murderers of Hiram. These three ruffians, who, when the Builder seeks to leave his temple, strike him with the tools of his own Craft until finally they slay him and bring the temple down in destruction upon their own heads, symbolize the three expressions of our own lower natures which are in truth the murderers of the good within ourselves. These three may be called thought, desire, and action. When purified and transmuted they are three glorious avenues through which may manifest the great life power of the three kings, the glowing builders of the Cosmic Lodge manifesting in this world as spiritual thought, constructive emotion, and useful daily labor in the various places and positions where we find ourselves while carrying on the Master's work. These three form the Flaming Triangle which glorifies every living Mason, but when crystallized and perverted they form a triangular prison through which the light cannot shine and the Life is forced to languish in the dim darkness of despair, until man himself through his higher understanding liberates the energies and powers which are indeed the builders and glorifiers of his Father's House.

Now let us consider how these three fiery kings of the dawn became, through perversion of their manifestation by man, the ruffians who murdered Hiram - the energizing powers of cosmos which course through the blood of every living being, seeking to beautify and perfect the temple they would build according to the plan laid down on the tracing board by the Master Architect of the universe. First in the mind is one of the three kings, or rather we shall say a channel through which he manifests; for King Solomon is the power of mind which, perverted, becomes a destroyer who tears down with the very powers which nourish and build. The right application of thought, when seeking the answer to the cosmic problem of destiny, liberates man's spirit which soars above the concrete through that wonderful power of mind, with its dreams and its ideals.

When man's thoughts rise upon the wings of aspiration, when he pushes back the darkness with the strength of reason and logic, then indeed the builder is liberated from his dungeon and the light pours in, bathing him with life and power. This light enables us to seek more clearly the mystery of creation and to find with greater certainty our place in the Great Plan, for as man unfolds his bodies he gains talents with which he can explore the mysteries of Nature and search for the hidden workings of the Divine. Through these powers the Builder is liberated and his consciousness goes forth conquering and to conquer. These higher ideals, these spiritual concepts, these altruistic, philanthropic, educative applications of thought power glorify the Builder; for they give the power of expression and those who can express themselves are free. When man can mold his thoughts, his emotions, and his actions into faithful expressions of his highest ideals then liberty is his, for ignorance is the darkness of Chaos and knowledge is the light of Cosmos.

In spite of the fact that many of us live apparently to gratify the desires of the body and as servants of the lower nature, still there is within each of us a power which may remain latent for a great length of time. This power lives eternities perhaps, and yet at some time during our growth there comes a great yearning for freedom, when, having discovered that the pleasures of sense gratification are eternally elusive and unsatisfying, we make an examination of ourselves and begin to realize that there are greater reasons for our being. It is sometimes reason, sometimes suffering, sometimes a great desire to be helpful, that brings out the first latent powers which show that one long wandering in the darkness is about to take the path that leads to Light. Having lived life in all its experiences, he has learned to realize that all the manifestations of being, all the various experiences through which he passes, are steps leading in one direction; that, consciously or unconsciously, all souls are being led to the portico of the temple where for the first time they see and realize the glory of Divinity. It is then that they understand the age-old allegory of the martyred Builder and feel his power within themselves crying out from the prison of materiality. Nothing else seems worth while; and, regardless of cost, suffering, or the taunts of the world, the candidate slowly ascends the steps that lead to the temple eternal. The reason that governs Cosmos he does not know, the laws which mold his being he does not realize, but he does know that somewhere behind the veil of human ignorance there is an eternal light toward which step by step he must labor. With his eyes fixed on the heavens above and his hands clasped in prayer he passes slowly as a candidate up the steps. In fear and trembling, yet with a divine realization of good, he raps on the door and awaits in silence the answer from within.

CHAPTER III

THE ENTERED APPRENTICE

There are three grand steps in the unfoldment of the human soul before it completes the dwelling place of the spirit. These have been caged respectively youth, manhood, and old age; or, as the Mason would say, the Entered Apprentice, the Fellow Craft, and the Master Builder. All life passes through these three grand stages of human consciousness. They can be listed as the man on the outside looking in, the man going in, and the man inside. The path of human life is governed as all things are by the laws of analogy, and as at birth we start our pilgrimmage through youth, manhood, and old age, so the spiritual consciousness of man in his cosmic path of unfoldment passes from unconsciousness to perfect consciousness in the Grand Lodge of the universe. Before the initiation of the Entered Apprentice degree can be properly understood and appreciated, certain requirements must be considered, not merely those of the physical world but also those of the spiritual world.

The Mason must realize that his true initiation is a spiritual and not a physical ritual, and that his initiation into the living temple of the spiritual hierarchy regulating Freemasonry may not occur until years after he has taken the physical degree, or spiritually he may be a Grand Master before he comes into the world. There are probably few instances in the history of Freemasonry where the spiritual ordination of the aspiring seeker took place at the same time as the physical initiation, because the true initiation depends upon the cultivation of certain soul qualities - an individual and personal matter which is left entirely to the volition of the mystic Mason and which he must carry out in silence and alone.

The court of the tabernacle of the ancient Jews was divided into three parts: the outer court, the holy place, and the most Holy of Holies. These three divisions represent the three grand divisions of human consciousness. The degree of Entered Apprentice is acquired when the student signifies his intention to take the rough ashlar which he cuts from the quarry and prepares for the truing of the Fellow Craft.

In other words, the first degree is really one of preparation; it is a material step dealing with material things, for all spiritual life must be raised upon a material foundation.

Seven is the number of the Entered Apprentice as it relates to the seven liberal arts and sciences, and these are the powers with which the Entered Apprentice must labor before he is worthy to go onward into the more elevated and advanced degrees. They are much mistaken who believe that they can reach the spiritual planes of Nature without first passing through and molding matter into the expression of spiritual power; for the first stage in the growth of a Master Mason is mastery of the concrete condition of life and the developments of sense centers which will later become channels for the expression of spiritual truths.

All growth is a gradual procedure carried on in an orderly, masterly way, as exemplified by the opening and closing of a lodge. The universe is divided into planes and these planes are divided from each other by the rates of vibration which pass through them. As the spiritual consciousness progresses through the chain, the lower lose connection with it when it has raised itself above their level, until finally only the Grand Masters are capable of remaining in session, and unknown even to the Master Mason it finally passes back again to the spiritual hierarchy from which it came.

Action is the keynote of the Entered Apprentice lodge. All growth is the result of exercise and the intensifying of vibratory rates. It is through exercise that the muscles of the human body are strengthened; it is through the seven liberal arts and sciences that the human mind receives certain impulses which, in turn, stimulate internal centers of consciousness. These centers of consciousness, through still greater development, will later give fuller expression to these inner powers; but the Entered Apprentice has for his first duty the awakening of these powers, and, like the youth of whom he is a symbol, his ideals and labors must be tied closely to concrete things. For him both points of the compasses are under the square; for him the reasons which manifest through the heart and mind - the two polarities of expression are darkened and concealed beneath the square which measures the block of bodies. He knows not the reason why; his work is to follow the directions of those whose knowledge is greater than his own; but as the result of the application of energies, through action and reaction he slowly builds and evolves the powers of discrimination and the strength of character which mark the Fellow Craft degree.

It is obvious that the rough ashlar symbolizes the body. It also represents cosmic root substance which is taken out of the quarry of the universe by the first expressions of intelligence and molded by them into ever finer and more perfect lines until finally it becomes the perfect stone for the Builder's temple.

How can emotion manifest save through form? How can mind manifest until the intricately evolved brain cells of matter have raised their organic quality to form the ground-work upon which other things may be based? All students of human nature realize that every expression of man depends upon organic quality; that in every living thing this differs; and that the fineness of this matter is the certain indication of growth - mental, physical or spiritual.

True to the doctrines of his Craft, the Entered Apprentice must beautify his temple. He must build within himself by his actions, by the power of his hand and the tools of his Craft, certain qualities which make possible his initiation into the higher degrees of the spiritual lodge.

We know that the cube block is symbolic of the tomb. It is also well known that the Entered Apprentice is incapable of rolling away the stone or of transmuting it into a greater or higher thing; but it is his privilege to purify and glorify that stone and begin the great work of preparing it for the temple of his King.

Few realize that since the universe is made up of individuals in various stages of development, responsibility is consequently individual, and everything which man wishes to gain he must himself build and maintain. If he is to use his finer bodies for the purpose for which they were intended, he must treat them well, that they may be good and faithful servants in the great work he is preparing for.

The quarries represent the limitless powers of natural resources. They are symbolic of the practically endless field of human opportunity; they symbolize the cosmic substances from which man must gather the stones for his temple. At this stage in his growth, the Entered Apprentice is privileged to gather the stones which he wishes to true during his progress through the lodge, for at this point he symbolizes the youth who is choosing his life work. He represents the human ego who in the dawn of time gathered many blocks and cubes and broken stones from the Great Quarry. These rough and broken stones that as yet will not fit into anything are the partially evolved powers and senses with which he labors. In the first state he must gather these materials, and those who have not gathered them can never true them. During the involuntary period of human consciousness, the Entered Apprentice in the Great Lodge was man, who labored with these rough blocks, seeking the tools and the power with which to true them . As he evolves down through the ages, he gains the tools and cosmically passes on to the degree of Fellow Craft where he trues his ashlar in harmony with the plans upon the Master's tracing board. This rough, uncut ashlar has three dimensions, representative of the three ruffians who at this stage are destroyers of the fourth dimensional life concealed within the ugly, ill-shaped stone.

The lost key of the Entered Apprentice is service. Why, he may not ask; when, he does not know. His work is to do, to act, to express himself in some way - constructively if possible, but destructively rather than not at all. Without action, he loses his great work; without tools, which symbolize the body, he cannot act in an organized manner. Consequently, it is necessary to master the arts and sciences which place in his hands intelligent tools for the expression of energy. Beauty is the keynote to his ideal. With his concrete ideals he must beautify all with which he comes in contact, so that the works of his hand may be acceptable in the eyes of the Great Architect of the Universe.

His daily life, in home, business, and society, together with the realization of the fundamental unity of each with all, form the base upon which the aspiring candidate may raise a greater superstructure. In truth he must live the life, the result of which is the purification of his body, so that the more attenuated forces of the higher degrees may express themselves through the finer sensitivity of the receiving pole within himself. When he reaches this stage in his growth, he is spiritually worthy to consider advancement into a higher degree. This advancement is not the result of election or ballot, but is an automatic process in which, having sensitized his consciousness by his life, he thereby attunes himself to the next succeeding plane of expression. All initiation is the result of adjustments of the evolving life to the physical, emotional, and mental planes of consciousness through which it passes.

We may now consider the spiritual requirements of one who feels that he would mystically correlate himself with that great spiritual fraternity which, concealed behind the exoteric rite, forms the living power of the Entered Apprentice lodge:

1. It is essential that the Entered Apprentice should have studied sufficiently the subject of anatomy to have at least a general idea of the physical body, for the entire

degree is based upon the mystery of form. The human body is the highest manifestation of form which he is capable of analyzing. Consequently, he must devote himself to the study of his own being and its mysteries and complexities.

2. The Entered Apprentice must realize that his body is the living temple of the living God and treat it accordingly; for when he abuses or mistreats it he breaks the sacred obligations which he must assume before he can ever hope to understand the true mysteries of the Craft. The breaking of his pact with the higher Life evolving within himself unfailingly invokes the retributive agencies of Nature.

3. He must study the problem of the maintenance of bodies through food, clothing, breathing, and other necessities, as all of these are important steps in the Entered Apprentice lodge. Those who eat immoderately, dress improperly, and use only about one-third of their lung capacity can never have the physical efficiency necessary for the fullest expression of the higher Life.

4. He must grow physically and in the expression of concrete things. Human relationships must be idealized at this time, and he must seek to unfold all unselfish qualities which are necessary for the harmonious working of the Mason and his fellow men on the physical plane of Nature.

5. He must seek to round off all inequalities. He can best do this by balancing his mental and physical organisms through the application and study of the seven liberal arts and sciences.

Until he is relatively master of these principles on the highest plane within his own being, he cannot hope spiritually to attract to himself, through the qualities of his own character, the life-giving ray of the Fellow Craft. When he reaches this point, however, he is spiritually ready to hope for membership in a more advanced degree.

The Mason must realize that his innermost motives are the index of his real self, and those who allow social position, financial or business considerations or selfish and materialistic ideals, to lead them into the Masonic Brotherhood have thereby automatically separated themselves from the Craft. They can never do any harm to Freemasonry by joining because they cannot get in. Ensconced within the lodge, they may feel that they have deceived the Grand Master of the Universe, but when the spiritual lodge meets to carry on the true work of the Craft, they are disqualified and absent. Watch fobs, lapel badges, and other insignia do not make Masons; neither does the ritual ordain them. Masons are evolved through the self-conscious effort to live up to the highest ideals within themselves; their lives are the sole insignia of their rank, greater by far than any visible, tangible credential.

Bearing this in mind, it is possible for the unselfish, aspiring soul to become spiritually and liberally vouched for by the centers of consciousness as an Entered Apprentice. It means he has taken the first grand step on the path of personal liberation. He is now symbolized as the child with the smiling face, for with the simplicity of a child he places himself under the protection of his great spiritual Father, willing and glad to obey each of His commands. Having reached this point and having done the best it was possible for him to do, he is in position to hope that the powers that be, moving in their mysterious manner, may find him worthy to undertake the second great step in spiritual liberation.

CHAPTER IV

THE FELLOW CRAFT

Life manifests not only through action on the physical plane, but through human emotion and sentiment. This is the type of energy taken up by the student when he starts his labors in the Fellow Craft. From youth with its smiling face, he passes on to the greater responsibilities of manhood.

On the second step of the temple stands a soldier dressed in shining armor, but his sword is sheathed and a book is in his hand. He is symbolic of strength, the energy of Mars, and the wonderful step in spiritual unfoldment which we know as Fellow Craft. Through each one of us course the fiery rays of human emotion, a great seething cauldron of power behind each expression of human energy. Like spirited horses chafing at the bit, like hounds eager for the chase, the emotional powers cannot be held in check, but break the walls of restraint and pour forth as fiery expressions of dynamic energy. This great principle of emotion we know as the second murderer of Hiram. Through the perversion of human emotions there comes into the world untold sorrow, which through reaction, manifests in the mental and physical bodies.

It is strange how divine powers may become perverted until each expression and urge becomes a ruffian and a murderer. The divine compassion of the gods manifests in this world of form very differently than in the realms of light. Divine compassion is energized by the same influxes as mortal passions and the lusts of earth. The spiritual light rays of

Cosmos - the Fire Princes of the Dawn - which seethe and surge through the unregenerate man, are the impulses which he perverts to murder and hate. The ceaseless power of Chaos, the seething pinwheel spirals of perpetual motion, whose majestic cadences are the music of the spheres, are energized by the same great power that man uses to destroy the highest and best. The same mystic power that keeps the planets in their orbits around the solar body, the same energy that keeps each electron spinning and whirling, the same energy that is building the temple of God, is now a merciless slave-driver which , unmastered and uncurbed, strikes the Compassionate One and sends him reeling backward into the darkness of his prison. Man does not listen to that little voice which speaks to him in ever loving, ever sorrowful tones. This voice speaks of the peace accompanying the constructive application of energy which he must chain if he would master the powers of creation. How long will it take King Hiram of Tyre, the warrior on the second step, symbolic of the Fellow Craft of the Cosmic Lodge, to teach mankind the lessons of self-mastery? The teacher can do it only as he daily depicts the miseries which are uncurbed appetites. The strength of man was not given to be used destructively but that he might build a temple worthy to be the dwelling place of the Great Architect of the universe. God is glorifying himself through the individualized portions of himself, and is slowly teaching these individualized portions to understand and glorify the whole.

The day has come when Fellow Craftsmen must know and apply their knowledge. The lost key to their grade is the mastery of emotion, which places the energy of the universe at their disposal. Man can only expect to be entrusted with great power by proving his ability to use it constructively and selflessly. When the Mason learns that the key to the warrior on the block is the proper application of the dynamo of living power, he has learned the mystery of his Craft. The seething energies of Lucifer are in his hands and before he may step onward and upward, he must prove his ability to properly apply energy. He must follow in the footsteps of his forefather, Tubal-Cain, who with the mighty strength of the war god hammered his sword into a plowshare. Incessant vigilance over thought, action, and desire is indispensable to those who wish to make progress in the unfolding of their own being, and the Fellow Craft's degree is the degree of transmutation. The hand that slays must lift the fallen, while the lips given to cursing must be taught to pray. The heart that hates must learn the mystery of compassion, as the result of a deeper and more perfect understanding of man's relation to his brother. The firm, kind hand of spirit must curb the flaming powers of emotion with an iron grip. In the realization and application of these principles lies the key of the Fellow Craft.

In this degree, the two points of the compass (one higher than the other), symbolize the heart and mind, and with the expression of the higher emotions the heart point of the compass is liberated from the square, which is an instrument used to measure the block of matter and therefore symbolizes form.

A large percentage of the people of the world at the present time are passing through, spiritually, the degree of the Fellow Craft, with its five senses. The sense perceptions come under the control of the emotional energies, therefore the development of the senses is necessary to the constructive expression of the Fellow Craft power. Man must realize that all the powers which his many years of need have earned for him have come in order that through them he may liberate more fully the prisoner within his own being. As the Fellow Craft degree is the middle of the three, the spiritual duty of each member is to reach the point of poise or balance, which is always secured between extremes. The mastery of expression is also to be found in this degree. The keywords of the Fellow Craft may be briefly defined as compassion, poise, and transmutation.

In the Fellow Craft degree is concealed the dynamo of human life. The Fellow Craft is the worker with elemental fire, which it is his duty to transmute into spiritual light. The heart is the center of his activity and it is while in this degree that the human side of the nature with its constructive emotions should be brought out and emphasized. But all of these expressions of the human heart must become transmuted into the emotionless compassion of the gods, who despite the suffering of the moment, gaze down upon mankind and see that it is good.

When the candidate feels that he has reached a point where he is able to manifest every energizing current and fire-flame in a constructive, balanced manner and has spiritually lifted the heart sentiments of the mystic out of the cube of matter, he may then expect that the degree of Master Mason is not far off, and so may look forward eagerly to the time of his spiritual ordination into the higher degree. He should now study himself and realize that he cannot receive promotion into the spiritual lodge until his heart is attuned to a superior, spiritual influx from the causal planes of consciousness.

The following requirements are necessary before the student can spiritually say that he is a member of the ancient and accepted rite of the Fellow Craft:

1. The mastery of emotional outbreaks of all kinds, poise under trying conditions, kindness in the face of unkindness, and simplicity with its accompanying power. These points show that the seeker is worthy of being taught by a Fellow Craftsman.

2. The mastery of the animal energies, the curbing of passion and desire, and the control of the lower nature mark the faithful attempts on the part of the student to be worthy of the Fellow Craft.

3. The understanding and mastery of the creative forces, the consecration of them to the unfolding of the spiritual nature, and a proper understanding of their physical application, are necessary steps at this stage of the student's growth.

4. The transmutation of personal affection into impersonal compassion shows that the Fellow Craftsman truly understands his duties and is living in a manner worthy of his order. Personalities cannot bind the true second degree member, for having raised one point of the compasses he now realizes that all personal manifestations are governed by impersonal principles.

5. At this point the candidate consecrates the five senses to the study of human problems with the unfolding of sense centers as the motive; for he realizes that the five senses are keys, the proper application of which will give him material for spiritual transmutation if he will apply to them the common divisor of analogy.

The Entered Apprentice may be termed a materialistic degree. The Fellow Craft is religious and mystical, while the Master Mason is occult or philosophical. Each of these is a degree in the unfoldment of a connected life and intelligence, revealing in ever fuller expression the gradual liberation of the Master from the triangular cell of threefold negation which marks the early stage of individualization.

CHAPTER V

THE MASTER MASON

On the upper steps of spiritual unfoldment stands the Master Mason, who spiritually represents the graduate from the school of esoteric learning. In the ancient symbols he is represented as an old man leaning upon a staff, his long white beard upon his chest, and his deep, piercing eyes sheltered by the brows of a philosopher. He is in truth old, not in years, but in wisdom and understanding, which are the only true measurement of age. Through years and lives of labor he has found the staff of life and truth upon which he leans. He no longer depends upon the words of others but upon the still voice that speaks from the heart of his own being. There is no more glorious position that a man may hold than that of a Master Builder, who has risen by labor through the degrees of human consciousness. Time is the differentiation of eternity devised by man to measure the passage of human events. On the spiritual planes of Nature it is the space or distance between the stages of spiritual growth and hence is not measurable by material means. Many a child comes into this world a Grand Master of the Masonic School, while many a revered and honored brother passes silently to rest without having gained admittance to its gate. The Master Mason is one whose life is full, pressed down and brimming over with the experience he has gained in his slow pilgrimage up the winding stairs.

The Master Mason embodies the power of the human mind, that connecting link which binds heaven and earth together in an endless chain. His spiritual light is greater because he has evolved a higher vehicle for its expression. Above even constructive action and emotion soars the power of thought which swiftly flies on wings to the source of Light. The mind is the highest form of his human expression and he passes into the great darkness of the inner room illuminated only by the fruits of reason. The glorious privileges of a Master Mason are in keeping with his greater knowledge and wisdom. From the student he has blossomed forth as the teacher; from the kingdom of those who follow he has joined that little group who must always lead the way. For him the Heavens have opened and the Great Light has bathed him in its radiance. The Prodigal Son, so long a wanderer in the regions of darkness, has returned again to his Father's house. The voice speaks from the Heavens, its power thrilling the Master until his own being seems filled with its divinity, saying, "This is my beloved Son, in whom I am well pleased." The ancients taught that the sun was not a source of light, life, or power, but a medium through which life and light were reflected into physical substance. The Master Mason is in truth a sun, a great reflector of light, who radiates through his organism, purified by ages of preparation, the glorious power which is the light of the Lodge. He, in truth, has become the spokesman of the Most High. He stands between the glowing fire light and the world. Through him passes Hydra, the great snake, and from its month there pours to man the light of God. His symbol is the rising sun, for in him the globe of day has indeed risen in all its splendor from the darkness of the night, illuminating the immortal East with the first promise of approaching day.

With a sigh the Master lays aside his tools. For him the temple is nearing completion, the last stones are being placed, and he slakes his lime with a vague regret as he sees dome and minaret rise through the power of his handiwork. The true Master does not long for rest, and as he sees the days of his labor close, a sadness weighs upon his heart. Slowly the brothers of his Craft leave him, each going his respective way; and, climbing step by step, the Master stands alone on the pinnacle of the temple. One stone must yet be placed, but this he cannot find. Somewhere it lies concealed. In prayer he kneels, asking the powers that be to aid him in his search. The light of the sun shines upon him and bathes him in a splendor celestial. Suddenly a voice speaks from the Heavens, saying, "The temple is finished and in my faithful Master is found the missing stone."

Both points of the compasses are now lifted from under the square. The divine is liberated from its cube; heart and mind alike are liberated from the symbol of mortality, and as emotion and thought they unite for the glorification of the greatest and the highest. Then the Sun and Moon are united and the Hermetic Degree is consummated.

The Master Mason is afforded opportunities far beyond the reach of ordinary man, but he must not fail to realize that with every opportunity comes a cosmic responsibility. It is worse by far to know and not to do than never to have known at all. He realizes that the choice of avoiding responsibility is no longer his and that for him all problems must be met and solved. The only joy in the heart of the Master is the joy of seeing the fruits of his handiwork. It can be truly said of the Master that through suffering he has learned to be glad, through weeping he has learned to smile, and through dying he has learned to live. The purification and probationship of his previous degrees have so spiritualized his being that he is in truth a glorious example of God's Plan for His children. The greatest sermon he can preach, the greatest lesson he can teach, is that of standing forth a living proof of the Eternal Plan. The Master Mason is not ordained: he is the natural product of cause and effect, and none but those who live the cause can produce the effect. The Master Mason, if he be truly a Master, is in communication with the unseen powers that move the destinies of life. As the Eldest Brother of the lodge, he is the spokesman for the spiritual hierarchies of his Craft. He no longer follows the direction of others, but on his own tracing board he lays out the plans which his brothers are to follow. He realizes this, and so lives that every line and plan which he gives out is inspired by the divine within himself. His glorious opportunity to be a factor in the growth of others comes before all else. At the seat of mercy he kneels, a faithful servant of the Highest within himself and worthy to be given control over the lives of others by having first controlled himself.

Much is said concerning the loss of the Master's Word and how the seekers go out to find it but bring back only substitutes. The true Master knows that those who go out can never find the secret trust. He alone can find it who goes within. The true Master Builder has never lost the Word but has cherished it in the spiritual locket of his own being. From those who have the eyes to see, nothing is concealed; to those who have the right to know, all things are open books. The true

Word of the three Grand Masters has never been concealed from those who have the right to know it nor has it ever been revealed to those who have not prepared a worthy shrine to contain it. The Master knows, for he is a Temple Builder. Within the setting of his own bodies, the Philosopher's Stone is placed; for in truth it is the heart of the Phoenix, that strange bird which rises with renewed youth from the ashes of its burned body. When the Master's heart is as pure and white as the diamond that he wears, he will then become a living stone- the crown jewel in the diadem of his Craft.

The Word is found when the Master himself is ordained by the living hand of God, cleansed by living water, baptized by living fire, a Priest-King after the Order of Melchizedek, who is above the law.

The great work of the Master Mason can be called the art of balance. To him is given the work of balancing the triangle that it may blaze forth with the glory of the Divine Degree. The triple energies of thought, desire, and action must be united in a harmonious blending of expression. He holds in his hands the triple keys; he wears the triple crown of the ancient Magus, for he is in truth the King of heaven, earth, and hell. Salt, sulphur, and mercury are the elements of his work and with the philosophical mercury he seeks to blend all powers to the glorifying of one end.

Behind the degree of Master Mason, there is another not known to earth. Far above him stretch other steps concealed by the blue veil which divides the seen from the unseen. The true Brother knows this, therefore he works with an end in view far above the concept of mortal mind. He seeks to be worthy to pass behind that veil and join that band who, unhonored and unsung, carry the responsibilities of human growth. His eyes are fixed forever on the Seven Stars which shine down from somewhere above the upper rung of the ladder. With hope, faith, and charity he climbs the steps, and whispering the Master's Word to the Keeper of the Gates, passes on behind the veil. It is then, and then only, that a true Mason is born. Only behind this veil does the mystic student come into his own. The things which we see around us are but forms-promises of a thing unnamed, symbols of a truth unknown. It is in the spiritual temple built without the voice of workmen or the sound of hammer that the true initiation is given, and there, robed in the simple lambskin of a purified body, the student becomes a Master Mason, chosen out of the world to be an active worker in the name of the Great Architect. It is there alone, unseen by mortal eyes, that the Greater Degrees are given and there the soul radiating the light of Spirit becomes a living; star in the blue canopy of the Masonic lodge.

TRANSMUTATION

Masonry is eternal truth, personified, idealized, and yet made simple. Eternal truth alone can serve it. Virtue is its priest, patience its warden, illumination its master. The world cannot know this, however, save when Masons in their daily life prove that it is so. Its truth is divine, and is not to be desecrated or defamed by the thoughtlessness of its keepers. Its temple is a holy place, to be entered in reverence. Material thoughts and material dissensions must be left without its gate. They may not enter. Only the pure of heart, regenerated and transmuted, may pass the sanctity of its veil. The schemer has no place in its ranks, nor the materialist in its shrine; for Masons walk on hallowed ground, sanctified by the veneration of ages. Let the tongue be stilled, let the heart be stilled, let the mind be stilled. In reverence and in the silence, stillness shall speak: the voice of stillness is the voice of the Creator. Show your light and your power to men, but before God what have you to offer, save in humility? Your robes, your tinsel, and your jewels mean naught to Him, until your own body and soul, gleaming with the radiance of perfection, become the living ornaments of your Lodge.

THE PRESENCE OF THE MASTER

The Mason believes in the Great Architect, the living keystone of creation's plan, the Master of all Lodges, without whose spirit there is no work. Let him never forget that the Master is near. Day and night let him feet the presence of the Supreme or Overshadowing One. The All-Seeing Eye is upon him. Day and night this great Orb measures his depths, seeing into his innermost soul of souls, judging his life, reading his thoughts, measuring his aspirations, and rewarding his sincerity. To this All-Seeing One he is accountable; to none other must he account. This Spirit passes with him out of the Lodge and measures the Mason in the world. This Spirit is with him when he buys and sells. It is with him in his home. By the light of day and by the darkness of night it judges him. It hears each thoughtless word. It is the silent witness to every transaction of life, the silent Partner of every man. By the jury of his acts, each man is judged. Let every Mason know that his obligations include not only those within the narrow Lodge, bordered by walls of stone and brick, but those in the Great Lodge, walled only by the dome of heaven. The Valley of Jehoshaphat waits for him who is false to any creature, as surely as it waited for the breakers of the Cosmic oath.

CHAPTER VI

THE QUALIFICATIONS OF A TRUE MASON

Every true Mason has come into the realization that there is but one Lodge - that is, the Universe - and but one Brotherhood, composed of everything that moves or exists in any of the planes of Nature. He realizes that the Temple of Solomon is really the Temple of the Solar Man -Sol-Om-On - the King of the Universe manifesting through his three primordial builders. He realizes that his vow of brotherhood and fraternity is universal, and that mineral, plant, animal, and man are all included in the true Masonic Craft. His duty as an elder brother to all the kingdoms of Nature beneath him is well understood by the true Craftsman, who would rather die than fail in this, his great obligation. He has dedicated his life upon the altar of his God and is willing and glad to serve the lesser through the powers he has gained from the greater. The mystic Mason, in building the eyes that see behind the apparent ritual, recognizes the oneness of life manifesting through the diversity of form.

The true disciple of ancient Masonry has given up forever the worship of personalities. With his greater insight, he realizes that all forms and their position in material affairs are of no importance to him compared to the life which is evolving within. Those who allow appearances or worldly expressions to deter them from their self-appointed tasks are failures in Masonry, for Masonry is an abstract science of spiritual unfoldment. Material prosperity is not the measure of soul growth. The true Mason realizes that behind these diverse forms there is one connected Life Principle, the spark of God in all living things. It is this Life which he considers when measuring the worth of a brother. It is to this Life that he appeals for a recognition of spiritual Unity. He realizes that it is the discovery of this spark of Unity which makes him a conscious member of the Cosmic Lodge. Most of all, he must learn to understand that this divine spark shines out as brightly from the body of a foe as it does from the dearest friend. The true Mason has learned to be divinely impersonal in thought, action, and desire.

The true Mason is not creed-bound. He realizes with the divine illumination of his lodge that as Mason his religion must be universal: Christ, Buddha or Mohammed, the name means little, for he recognizes only the light and not the bearer. He worships at every shrine, bows before every altar, whether in temple, mosque or cathedral, realizing with his truer understanding the oneness of all spiritual truth. All true Masons know that they only are heathen who, having great ideals, do not live up to them. They know that all religions are but one story told in diverse ways for peoples whose ideals differ but whose great purpose is in harmony with Masonic ideals. North, east, south and west stretch the diversities of human thought, and while the ideals of man apparently differ, when all is said and the crystallization of form with its false concepts is swept away, one basic truth remains: all existing things are Temple Builders, laboring for a single end. No true Mason can be narrow, for his Lodge is the divine expression of all broadness. There is no place for little minds in a great work.

The true Mason must develop the powers of observation. He must seek eternally in all the manifestations of Nature for the things which he has lost because he failed to work for them. He must become a student of human nature and see in those around him the unfolding and varying expressions of one connected spiritual Intelligence. The great spiritual ritual of his lodge is enacted before him in every action of his fellow man. The entire Masonic initiation is an open secret, for anyone can see it played out on the city street corners as well as in the untracked wilderness. The Mason has sworn that every day he will extract from life its message for him and build it into the temple of his God. He seeks to learn the things which will make him of greater service in the Divine Plan, a better instrument in the hands of the Great Architect, who is laboring eternally to unfold life through the medium of living things. The Mason realizes, moreover, that his vows, taken of his own free will and accord, give him the divine opportunity of being a living tool in the hands of a Master Workman.

The true Master Mason enters his lodge with one thought uppermost in his mind: "How can I, as an individual, be of greater use in the Universal Plan? What can I do to be worthy to comprehend the mysteries which are unfolded here? How can I build the eyes to see the things which are concealed from those who lack spiritual understanding?" The true Mason is supremely unselfish in every expression and application of the powers that have been entrusted to him. No true Brother seeks anything for himself, but unselfishly labors for the good of all. No person who assumes a spiritual obligation for what he can get out of it is worthy of applying for the position even of water-carrier. The true Light can come only to those who, asking nothing, gladly give all to it.

The true brother of the Craft, while constantly striving to improve himself, mentally, physically, and spiritually through the days of his life, never makes his own desires the goal for his works. He has a duty and that duty is to fit into the plans of another. He must be ready at any hour of the day or night to drop his own ideals at the call of the Builder. The work must be done and he has dedicated his life to the service of those who know the bonds of neither time nor space. He must be ready at any moment's notice and his life should be turned into preparing himself for that call which may come when he least expects it. The Master Mason knows that those most useful to the Plan are those who have gained the most from the practical experiences of life. It is not what goes on within the tiled lodge which is the basis of his greatness, but rather the way in which he meets the problems of daily life. The true Masonic student is known by his brotherly actions and common sense.

Every Mason knows that a broken vow brings with it a terrible penalty. Let him also realize that failure to live mentally, spiritually, and morally up to one's highest ideals constitutes the greatest of all broken oaths. When a Mason swears that he will devote his life to the building of his Father's house and then defiles his living temple through the perversion of mental power, emotional force, and active energy, he is breaking a vow which imposes not hours but ages of misery. If he is worthy to be a Mason, he must be great enough to restrain the lower side of his own nature which is daily murdering his Grand Master. He must realize that a misdirected life is a broken vow and that daily service, purification, and the constructive application of energy is a living invocation which builds within and draws to him the power of the Creator. His life is the only prayer acceptable in the eyes of the Most High. An impure life is a broken trust; a destructive action is a living curse; a narrow mind is a strangle-cord around the throat of God.

All true Masons know that their work is not secret, but they realize that it must remain unknown to all who do not live the true Masonic life. Yet if the so-called secrets of Freemasonry were shouted from the housetops, the Fraternity would be absolutely safe; for certain spiritual qualities are necessary before the real Masonic secrets can be understood by the brethren themselves. Hence it is that the alleged "exposures" of Freemasonry, printed by the thousands and tens of thousands since 1730 down to the present hour, cannot injure the Fraternity. They reveal merely the outward forms and ceremonies of Freemasonry. Only those who have been weighed in the balance and found to be true, upright, and square have prepared themselves by their own growth to appreciate the inner meanings of their Craft. To the rest of their brethren within or without the lodge their sacred rituals must remain, as Shakespeare might have said, "Words, words, words." Within the Mason's own being is concealed the Power, which, blazing forth from his purified being, constitutes the Builder's Word. His life is the sole password which admits him to the true Masonic Lodge. His spiritual urge is the sprig of acacia which, through the darkness of ignorance, still proves that the spiritual fire is alight. Within himself he must build those qualities which will make possible his true understanding of the Craft. He can show the world only forms which mean nothing; the life within is forever concealed until the eye of Spirit reveals it.

The Master Mason realizes charity to be one of the greatest traits which the Elder Brothers have unfolded, which means not only properly regulated charity of the purse but charity in thought and action. He realizes that all the workmen are not on the same step, but wherever each may be, he is doing the best he can according to his light. Each is laboring with the tools that he has, and he, as a Master Mason, does not spend his time in criticizing but in helping them to improve their tools. Instead of blaming poor tools, let us always blame ourselves for having them. The Master Mason does not find fault; he does not criticize nor does he complain, but with malice towards none and charity towards all he seeks to be worthy of his Father's trust. In silence he labors, with compassion he suffers, and if the builders strike him as he seeks to work with them, his last word will be a prayer for them. The greater the Mason, the more advanced in his Craft, the more fatherly he grows, the walls of his Lodge broadening out until all living things are sheltered and guarded within the blue folds of his cape. From laboring with the few he seeks to assist all, realizing with his broader understanding the weaknesses of others but the strength of right.

A Mason is not proud of his position. He is not puffed up by his honor, but with a sinking heart is eternally ashamed of his own place, realizing that it is far below the standard of his Craft. The farther he goes, the more he realizes that he is standing on slippery places and if he allows himself for one moment to lose his simplicity and humility, a fall is inevitable. A true Mason never feels himself worthy of his Craft. A student may stand on the top of Fool's Mountain self-satisfied in his position , but the true Brother is always noted for his simplicity.

A Mason cannot be ordained or elected by ballot. He is evolved through ages of self-purification and spiritual transmutation. There are thousands of Masons who are brethren in name only, for their failure to exemplify the ideals of their Craft makes them unresponsive to the teachings and purpose of Freemasonry. The Masonic life forms the first key of the Temple and without this key, none of the doors can be opened. When this fact is better realized and lived, Freemasonry will awake, and speak the Word so long withheld. The speculative Craft will then become operative, and the Ancient Wisdom so long concealed will rise from the ruins of its temple as the greatest spiritual truth yet revealed to man.

The true Master Mason recognizes the value of seeking for truth wherever he can find it. It makes no difference if it be in the enemy's camp; if it be truth, he will go there gladly to secure it. The Masonic Lodge is universal; therefore all true Masons will seek through the extremities of creation for their Light. The true brother of the Craft knows and applies one great paradox. He must search for the high things in lowly places and find the lowly things in high places. The Mason who feels holier than his fellow man has raised a barrier around himself through which no light can pass, for the one who in truth is the greatest is the servant of all. Many brethren make a great mistake in building a wall around their secrets, for they succeed only in shutting out their own light. Their divine opportunity is at hand. The time has come when the world needs the Ancient Wisdom as never before. Let the Mason stand forth and by living the doctrines which he preaches show to his brother man the glory of his work. He holds the keys to truth; let him unlock the door, and with his life and not his words preach the doctrine which he has so long professed.

The Fatherhood of God and the Brotherhood of Man were united in the completion of the Eternal Temple, the Great Work, for which all things came into being and through which all shall glorify their Creator.

MASONS, AWAKE!

Your creed and your Craft demand the best that is in you. They demand the sanctifying of your life, the regeneration of your body, the purification of your soul, and the ordination of your spirit. Yours is the glorious opportunity; yours is the divine responsibility. Accept your task and follow in the footsteps of the Master Masons of the past, who with the flaming spirit of the Craft have illumined the world. You have a great privilege - the privilege of illumined labor. You may know the ends to which you work, while others must struggle in darkness. Your labors are not to be confined to the tiled Lodge alone, for a Mason must radiate the qualities of his Craft. Its light must shine in his home and in his business, glorifying his association with his fellow men. In the Lodge and out of the Lodge, the Mason must represent the highest fruitage of sincere endeavor.

EPILOGUE:
MOTIVE

What motive leads the Masonic candidate out of the world and up the winding stairway to the light? He alone can truly know, for in his heart is hidden the motive of his works. Is he seeking the light of the East? Is he seeking wisdom eternal? Does he bring his life and offer it upon the altar of the Most High? Of all things, motive is most important. Though we fail again and again, it our motive be true, we are victorious. Though time after time we succeed, if our motive be unworthy, we have failed. Enter the temple in reverence, for it is in truth the dwelling place of a Great Spirit, the Spirit of Masonry. Masonry is an ordainer of kings. Its hand has shaped the destinies of worlds, and the perfect fruitage of its molding is an honest man. What nobler thing can be accomplished than the illumination of ignorance? What greater task is there than the joyous labor of service? And what nobler man can there be than that Mason who serves his Lights, and is himself a light unto his fellow men?

Milton Keynes UK
Ingram Content Group UK Ltd.
UKHW041005061024
2024UKWH00030B/71